The Adventures of Zoey and the Eight Planets & Pluto
AF488669

this book belongs to:

____

Summary

The story follows a curious little girl named Zoey who discovers a magical telescope in her backyard. Upon looking through it, she is transported on a colorful rocket ship to explore the eight planets of the solar system. Each planet introduces itself to Zoey, sharing unique characteristics and qualities. After visiting Mercury, Venus, Earth, Mars, Jupiter, Saturn, Uranus, and Neptune, Zoey returns home, grateful for her adventure. That night, she looks up at the stars, cherishing the experience and hoping to visit the planets again in her dreams.

Resource Page

Zoey was a curious little girl with bright eyes and a big imagination. One day, she found a magical telescope in her backyard. "I wonder what I'll see!" she said, peering into the lens.

As soon as Zoey looked through the telescope, she was whisked away on a colorful rocket ship! "Wow, I'm going to explore the planets!" Zoey cheered as she zoomed through space.

Did you know?
The Moon is Earth's only natural satellite and the fifth largest moon in the solar system.

First, Zoey landed on Mercury. "You're the closest to the Sun!" Zoey said. Mercury was tiny and very hot. "Be careful, Zoey," said Mercury, "I'm really warm because I'm so close to the Sun!"

Did you know?

Mercury speeds through space with 50km per second/31 miles per second.

Next, Zoey flew to Venus. Venus was bright
and beautiful, like a shining star. "I'm
covered in clouds that trap heat," Venus said.
"But I still love to shine bright in the sky!"

Did you know?

Venus is the second planet from the Sun
and is Earth's closest planetary neighbor.

Did you know?

Earth is our home planet.

After Earth, Zoey visited Mars. Mars was red and dusty. "I'm called the Red Planet because of my rusty color," Mars explained. "Maybe one day, people will visit me, too!"

Did you know?

Mars is the only planet where we've sent rovers to roam the alien landscape.

Zooming farther, Zoey reached Jupiter. Jupiter was huge with big, swirling clouds. "I'm the biggest planet!" Jupiter boomed. "I even have a big storm called the Great Red Spot!"

Did you know?

Jupiter is the largest of the planets, and its moon Ganymede is large too.

Next, Zoey traveled to Saturn.
Saturn was beautiful with shiny
rings made of ice and rock. "My
rings make me special," Saturn said
proudly. "Aren't they lovely?"

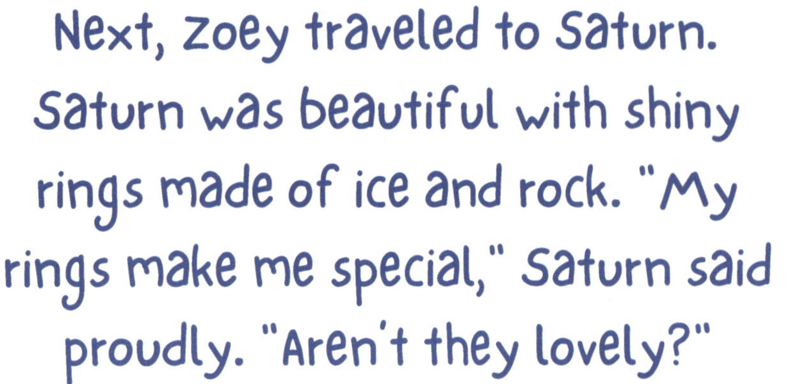

Did you know?

Saturn is a massive ball made mostly of
hydrogen and helium.

Zoey then found Uranus. Uranus was a chilly, light blue planet that spun on its side. "I'm different from the others because I tilt!" Uranus said with a wink.

Did you know?

Uranus was discovered in 1781 by astronomer William Herschel.

Finally, Zoey reached Neptune.
Neptune was deep blue and very
windy. "I'm the farthest planet
from the Sun," Neptune said with
a howl of wind. "I'm cold, but I'm
full of mysteries!"

Did you know?

Neptune is the only planet in our solar
system not visible to the naked eye.

Hold up! Let's get acquainted with little Pluto, the celestial cutie now classified as a dwarf planet since 2006.

Did you know?

Pluto is no longer considered a planet as per the definitions of astronomy, and now it comes under the category of "Dwarf Planet".

After visiting all eight planets, including Pluto
the dwarf planet, Zoey's rocket ship took her
back home. "that was the best adventure ever!"
Zoey said as she landed safely in her backyard.

That night, Zoey looked up at the stars and smiled. "Thank you, planets," she whispered. "I'll dream of you tonight and maybe one day, I'll visit again.

About the Author

Hello, I am C Brutus, I was born in Haiti in October 1992. Upon relocating to the United States, I pursued my education and embraced a diverse range of roles and accomplishments. Balancing the responsibilities of a devoted mother to two daughters and a supportive Navy wife, I handle my family duties with grace and resilience. In my professional life, I work with special education students, showcasing my dedication to inclusivity and education. Beyond the classroom, my love for learning and teaching led me to become a successful author. My collection includes various books like coloring books, activity books, and storybooks, all crafted to engage and inspire young minds. I am truly grateful for your support. A big thank you to my amazing customers for backing my small business endeavors.

Thank you!

C Brutus